Unsilent Night

Unsilent Night

Poetic Reflections on the Expressiveness of God

ANNETTE ANDERSEN

XULON PRESS

Xulon Press
2301 Lucien Way #415
Maitland, FL 32751
407.339.4217
www.xulonpress.com

Unless otherwise indicated, Scripture quotations are taken from the Holy Bible, New International Version®, NIV® Copyright ©1973, 1978, 1984, 2011 by Biblica, Inc.® Used by permission. All rights reserved worldwide.

Printed in the United States of America.

ISBN-13: 978-1-5456-7953-1

Dedicated to the One from Whom the blessing of all words flow. Thank you for coming for me.

Table of Contents

Preface

My original intent was for this book of poems to be of Christmas content only. God did express Himself to mankind that unusual night in ways both startling and beautiful. His speech has never stopped. He reveals Himself to each of us uniquely within the context of our everyday lives. So I have chosen to stretch a bit beyond that original intent. Poetry has been a major megaphone for me. I vividly remember the inner emotional explosion I experienced as a child upon my first exposure. It happened in a school classroom. That first stick of dynamite was written by the author, Edwin Markham and read as follows:

"He drew a circle that cut me out-
Heretic, rebel, a thing to flout.
But love and I had the wit to win.
We drew a circle that took him in."

Like the Grinch's heart did when he finally "got" Christmas, my little heart swelled two times its size (or was it ten?) when our teacher read it to us from one of our textbooks. I read it over and over that day. I just knew

I was going to grow up some day and march out and conquer all the hate in the world because the secret formula was right there in those few little lines of words. Powerful thing. Years have come and gone. Life experience has exposed the simplified-ness of Markham's words. Yet, many poems later (some my own) without having quite accomplished anything near that lofty goal, I can still feel the longing and hope for possibilities such as those inspired by his poem to be true...just like I felt on the day I first heard it. Since then, I've met and now know the Source of all words and of that kind of love. I know it to be true that to "know" Him is really the secret. My hope is that you might catch a glimpse of the magnificent One beyond the face in a manger whose hand is reaching up to touch your face. This is where your poem will begin. May some of these few words be part of that tender touch.

Chapter One

" *God crowds upon us from Sheol to the sea. He jostles our thoughts along the pathways in our brains. He hides in the bushes, jumping out in flames to startle us into seeing. He sequesters Himself in stables and swaddling so as to take us unawares. He veils Himself in flesh, the same flesh that drips into fingers at the end of my arms and sprouts into the hair of my head.*"

Virginia Owens

I was two or three years old in this furthest back memory of my childhood Christmases. I was sick with earaches and fever and my father was reassuring me that Santa would still come even if I did not feel good and could not fall asleep. One or two years later a little girl in a nightgown (me) pads into the living room late Christmas Eve night to find my mother rocking my baby sister. I voiced my very real concern to mom that she must not be doing this because Santa would not come if she were up. She smiled and sent me back to bed with reassurances that all would be well and the next morning it was. There was magic and mystery in the air even though my family did not talk about why. Whatever it was, it was delicious. I pretended one year beyond knowing the truth about Santa because I was reluctant to let the magic go. And somewhere in those years between believing and knowing better, another thing happened that softened the blow. A better and truer Santa introduced Himself to me. This One carried a bigger load of presents than my childhood Santa ever could. And this One contained enough mystery and magic within his persona for a lifetime. So I segued from childhood into adulthood almost without a bump between wonders. Delicious fantasy to an even more delicious reality. God right with me for always and always...not just for one time of the year. He has brought enough adventure that my nights have hardly been silent since. And still I lean in to listen with expectant ear.

Unsilent Night

Deep in this silent, routine night
the air is dark and cool and stars are sharp.
I wrap my cloak more closely still
and lean for warmth and light
away from shadows and the chill.

How could I know this normal night
my fold, the sky would soon explode
around my homespun cloak and flame
with unfamiliar song and light
and I would never see the same.

The dark is different since that night
though cloak and flame may warm me still.
I listen with expectant ear
and lean into a brighter light
since star and song and child appeared.

The Visitation

The eve you slipped through heaven's sphere
from her innocent womb, was anything but silent.
Your cry, confined in mortal sound, pierced
earth's long, quiet night…shattered our sleep.

Neither was the sky dark nor calm.
Beneath a blazing star, in lighted loft,
a choir of bright beings announced in song
and hovered near enough to startle sheep and men.

Behind the scenes, in minor key, but loud,
shadows screamed discordant sounds.
The earth became a stage, where voices
raised in conflict, raged or praised.

You do not change. Your ageless voice, relentless,
calls each by name. Resonates with love and grace.
And still our startled souls respond…some,
ambivalent and some, with rage or praise.

There is a popular event being propagated these days. A number of people meet at a given place and are broken up into groups. Each unit is given the same first clue to decipher in order to figure out a second destination where another clue will be found that will send them to the next one… and so on, until one group reaches the final destination first and wins the prize. I hear there is another game similar to the scavenger hunt that is also popular now. Because of technology, Geocaching is not limited to one group of people in one local setting . Both games have a similar theme. Search for clues, follow them, and find treasure. This longing for adventure…this yearning for there to be a search that calls for the best of the detective in each of us whose prize wows at the end of the day, is Divinely placed in our DNA. We snatch up the clues like candy and off we go searching for that final thing…something so satisfying that all our efforts fade to nothingness in comparison. Sometimes we get the clues wrong and wind up in the wrong place. We put our heads together. We go back to the clue and pick it apart, until the mystery reveals itself to us. The search is not meant to go on forever. It ends in a certain place at a certain time and there is a prize to be had.

Divinity was once delivered to us in a certain place at a certain time in the history of our cosmos. The clues to His coming were scattered throughout the Old Testament writings and spiritual seekers in that era pulled at the tape and wrappings with intrigue to get to the prize inside. It was not to be had for their era. Finally, at the appointed time, wrapped in the guise of humanity, the Gift was revealed and lay in a lowly wooden bed filled with straw surrounded by common things. It would be easy to miss the clues. But *once we recognize the prize in a personal way, in peace and wonder at this thing that outshines all others, we can lay down our search and accept the gift of Himself that He offers to us each.*

What Wisemen Know

Treasure.
That which is held in high esteem.
Dearly prized.
Desired .
Not always deserved.

You
my King, I house tremblingly.
Exquisite jewel
in so common a setting.
All other gems are
but reflections of You.

He Is

Like wisemen
I have chased a star
and hoped and searched
in distant night
for light to lead me near.

Like shepherds
I have heard a song
that called me in
from distant hills
to find a cave and child.

Like these
I've laid my gifts and staff
near mighty, humble, manger bed
and found this Childs' the gold, the song.
He is my journey's end.

Intrigue

Like a shepherd,
I hear singing.
I must know the words.

Like an angel,
I feel wonder.
I must express with song.

Like a wiseman,
I see light.
I must find its source.

Like a stable,
plain and empty.
I will welcome Him.

Always grateful,
Royal Presence.
Now You live within.

Guiding Star

Truth came…sweet and strong.
Reality in human form. Now,
stoop through doorways
of dark stable hearts.
Lift us from sleepy straw
beds with power and light,
blazing like the star.
Take us where You are.

"It seems, then," said Tirian, smiling himself, "that the Stable seen from within and the stable seen from without are two different places."

"Yes," said the Lord Digory. "Its inside is bigger than its outside."

"Yes," said Queen Lucy. "In our world too, a Stable once had something inside it that was bigger than our whole world."

This passage is from C.S. Lewis' book, *The Last Battle*. It is pulled from his story about the adventures of children who are transported magically into another land from ours. Lewis has woven the tale as such so that in one scene, he alludes to the stable of our Christmas narrative and we find it is possible for the characters in the tale to be outside the stable of Incarnation and only see a humble building. They have no idea what is contained within those wooden walls (like we often also do not) until they go inside. Some who step over the threshold are astounded by a fresh, new, beautiful world that is bigger than the one out of which they stepped; however, others who take that same step, see only a small wooden space filled with murky shadows and stinky straw. His point is that we need something supernatural to happen to our natural sight before we can "see" what (or Who) is really there. Some of Lewis' characters already had a personal experience with Aslan (the "Christ" in his tale) who gave them this new sight already. Some had not. Bequeathed awareness made all the difference in what each would find "inside." We need help from the One we come to see in order to "see." Then we need to stay until our new sight adjusts to His presence. The dark corners we have become accustomed to will light up in His brilliance.

And we will be able to see what we could not. It is a new way of experiencing love and then one another in the light of that. He will enable us to "come out" into the light and function in new ways for which we had no ability until He came for us and made us "able." The doorway for us starts in a stable. He didn't stay there. And neither will we if we go with Him. Our horizons will be enlarged right where we are and we will go out from the inside into a better place with Him leading the way.

Invitation

Come to my complacent stable
of wood, straw,
dirt, smells, and shadows.

Come, like one of us
as I've heard you once did.
Creator confined in safe swaddling.

Come, help me peek
beneath the cloths
Beyond a baby's guise and form.

Stay, til my eyes
adjust to Your brilliance
then lead me out
that I may live in light.

Anticipation

Oh holy night…
poised and tremulous
to host your Creator
you anticipate, (as I have)
His coming and the light.

Oh Holy One …
Near and resplendent.
You did not disappoint.
Now all my nights are holy
and all my days celebrate Your birth.

Transcendent Guest

He stoops to be born again
in tiny stables.
In the humble straw
of our lives He lays.

He comes to nourish anew
our hungry places.
In the empty mangers
of our lives He lays.

He lives to revive again
our deadened spaces.
In the stubble and wood
of our lives He lays.

He indwells to burn
then build again.
In the raised-up rooms
of our hearts He reigns.

Oh Holy Light

Do you see what I see?
One star streams through
light years of nights.
Beams through curtained
flesh and bone. Lights
each stable space.
All gold, scent, and gem
pale to shadowed heaps
beside this Royal Ray.
He is here now…
no longer hidden by night.
Oh Holy Light.

Chapter Two

Unable to grasp God's essence, we seek help in words. In names. In animal forms. In figures. In trees and flowers and summits and sources.

C.S. Lewis

My Friend the Pen

My pen is an old friend…
Comfortable and fine pointed.
A precise presence
with ink that never ends.

My pen is a new friend…
Mysterious and promising.
A bold endeavor
with unfamiliar bends.

My pen is an airplane…
swooping and diving.
Breaks sound barriers.
Makes my stomach leap.

My pen is a journey…
Determined and driven.
Headed somewhere
across a white desert
and I ride piggyback.
My friend, the pen.

Annette Andersen

Midwinter's Dream is a very personal poem. It is about me. And continues to be about me. It is about a handsome prince who brought springtime to this captive child who was frozen in a tomb of insecurity and fear. It is about each of us who need to be rescued from forces that are too strong for us. Jesus comes and spring comes for us. For me. For you.

Midwinter's Dream

You lie suspended under this thick quilt
that comes down cool and white and holds you still.
And though your heart beats steady as you dream
We may not see the greens and yellows there.

A warm alarm rings muffled in your ear
And Jesus calls your early morning name
and lifts and throws back this ice covering
and orders winter now give way to spring.

Ezekiel 36:26 I will give you a new heart and put a new
spirit in you; I will remove from you your heart of stone
and give you a heart of flesh.

Psalm 51:10 Create in me a pure heart, O God, and renew
a steadfast spirit within me.

John 7: 37 On the last and greatest day of the Feast, Jesus
stood and said in a loud voice, "If anyone is thirsty, let
him come to me and drink. Whoever believes in me, as the
scripture has said, streams of living water will flow from
within him."

In those days of hearing odd things, we lived in an old house that had a strange habit. Not one to be counted on… just an occasional, unnerving habit. Rarely, but sometimes, when the strong "Lion" winds of early March blew just so, we could hear horse sounds around one corner as moving air funneled fiercely through the eves outside. These were not the nickers of soft nosed friends. One dark night, as I read late in my corner, they came. And I made this attempt to harness a bit of my experience with them in words. When we re-sided the house, they never came back. I miss their mysterious spring visits. And I still wonder what they were up to.

Horses in the Wind

I've heard many unseemly travelers in the wind. Waves
are out there. They've rushed up against my windows

from distant unknown shores. But never have I
heard this strange thing. Never horses before. One just

swooped low and in shrieking neigh, threatened, I thought,
to crash through glass into my corner reading place.

I think there's more. I hear them rushing through
trees and were I to look out into the

dark and moving night, I'd not know which were
leaves and limbs or flowing manes and tails.

Herds of them! Wild, fierce forms like spirits of horses
ridden in wars or angered by man, not those

I knew as friends when young. I wonder who they're
searching for or if their eyes burn red in shadowed

coats of bronze or black. I yearn to peek beyond this thin
transparent glass but shall not reach and lift the curtain back

Dark Intent

How treacherous the bow,
the taunt string when
the arrow flung in fury
finds a single mark,
its bitter tip, a flint,
whose flame may burn,
without regret, a forest
or a person down.

Sleeping Grandfather

In this old wood chest from your house, I feel the worn
brown leather that still enfolds the faded license you used
for 80 years. I search for more. Past glasses, scratched,
your imprints pressed upon the lens, like on my sight
I search for something needed now and close my eyes.

I drag a match across the rough hewn years to light the
blackened lamp wick by your face and you are here. In
stolen moments warmth from winter's cold, I am unsure
which time this one might be, all the fields you plowed with
horse and team are crisscrossed deep in furrowed face asleep.

Pools form round your buckled rubber boots from melted snow
or my tears. Books pile high around your chair and One's well
worn. I yearn to hear its words in just your way. Now you sense
me near and quick, a weathered hand shoots up to cover being caught
like this again. This nap you steal in old chair between chores.
Beyond surprise to find me here, your eyes hold what

I knew before and warmly span the space and years
and seem to say that somehow, like before, you understand.
Stay I whisper as shadows veil the contours of your face.
The oil burns low and there's so much to say. What's true
has dimmed. I need a flag to set my furrow straight.
You touch my sight with fingertip. It is enough.
I close the old wood lid. You fade away.

25

"*Inner Fires*" was inspired by a gathering held every-Saturday night throughout the summer months called "*Stone Circle Poets.*" It is an unusual event unique to this northern Michigan region and has been going on for over 30 years. People who are interested in poetry, story telling, song writing or music, gather around a huge bonfire in an opening encircled by birch and poplar forests and large boulders scattered throughout the site. Amidst chairs, blankets and a roaring fire, guests either listen to or actively orate either one's own work or that of a favorite other. Musicians sometimes sing or play or both. All must be done from memory standing or walking about in the midst of the group by firelight. On the best nights, the sky is clear and starlit and breezes cause the canopy of trees surrounding the outer edges of the sphere to sing background melodies to our word offerings. For a few years, I both attended and even mustered up the courage to orate a few times. Out of those times came this poem.

Inner Fires

Behind, the night breathes and waits in cool
starlight to claim our warm intrusive glow. I
I see no heaving chest and yet outside this lucid
wreath of bright faces, all darkness moves and
sways and I bless the blanket between. Beyond,
some shadows tower and lean and toss bent heads
whose movements fling whispers that rush through
the rising, falling rhythms of yarns spun to listening
stars. We'll swear they're true!

We offer humble wood to keep these flames that
illuminate and guard our flickering stage where
words perchance at times are starter sparks that
shower out and light upon and catch at wood in
hearts. As coals, like children's tired but valiant
eyes, rubbed red but opened wide, begin to fade
and blink and fade, we'll take our inner fires out in
this night whose eager leaning form at circle's edge
we've held at bay and shunned by wood and words.

For many years, my husband and I have eagerly headed across Michigan's "Straights of Mackinac" bridge every fall to spend three idyllic weeks at LaBounty cottage on Lake Superior. Michigan shares this whimsical, temperamental, inland sea with Wisconsin, Minnesota and Canada. In 2001, the autumn colors of our vacation and of our homeland were changed forever. That September 11th, five days before we were to leave, tragedy struck our country. We went with heavy hearts and sheltered within LaBounty's strong old arms where good memories surrounded us like the warmth of the evening fires in her big stone fireplace. Friends and family came and went while we were there. This was good…we went on as best as we could with an undercurrent of loss and sadness ever in the shadows, poignant and sharp. Would we ever come back again? Where would our country be at this time next year? There was (and has proven true) a strong sense that something had changed forever.

It was raining on the day we had to leave. A deep and bittersweet appreciation for the gift of carefree freedom I had known all my life hovered in the late season chill and I wrapped it around me like an heirloom quilt that I needed to touch and feel once more…just a few more moments here…just a few more. I wrote this poem with our car packed and waiting. It was so hard to go.

Leaving Day

Spatters of raindrops
trickle down LaBounty's panes.
Traces of laughter and sorrow
run together down my soul,
a bittersweet stream of warmth
and pain. Sweet memories made
here glisten, then dissipate against
September's harsh frame. Sharp
sadness dampens the scene as I
leave to a different world than
I knew in innocent August.

October 15, 2001

Away

Tucked away all year in a corner
where anticipations stay, is September.
Wrapped in golden days, jackets and Superior air.

We wait "until" ... Ever expectant to open,
once again, the gift of Rock River...
the blessing of camp LaBounty.

Interior Designed

I don't know how to find You here where
doors are few and walls are not where
they should be. I grope for burnished knobs
too tall for me, and stumble on dark floors.
I reach to find my way to Your safe room.

Use Your hammer. Remake this space then,
like a lover, lead me across the threshold
to rooms warm with joy where hope hangs
for curtains and faith lies bright in woven
colors, soft yet solid beneath my bewildered feet.

Where patterned walls are frames for doors
whose low handles gleam to lead a reaching
child from night. Rebuild so dreams can leap,
like surprises, from closets onto maple floors
in filtered light. Raze, then rebuild a place
where I can find and want to live with You.

There are moments of awareness that are very personal glances from God . They don't come every day…though I wonder how often they may be all around us and we are too busy or preoccupied to notice that He is near. I know this is true of me. Once in awhile, our eyes meet…He is looking into mine and I am looking back…that is when magic happens as did that warm autumn day in Memorial Falls ravine, a little known miniature canyon in the upper peninsula of Michigan. We had it all to ourselves. The sun filtered through the brilliant maples…water cascaded… Mark and I lay on our backs looking up through the canopy just drinking it in. And I was suddenly "aware" that we were not alone. Fellow pilgrim, may you be able to notice His golden glances that are just for you. He waits and hopes.

Sightseers

Let down your hair.
I want to see the silent hues
hidden beneath the browns.
Reds almost too shy to shine
without a golden glance.

I am gazing at you now.
Scenic in simplicity, you rest
beneath a canopy whose greens
and yellows I designed that
charm as I am charmed .

I hear you think: "Who must this be
who wildly carved this scene from rock
in early days?" Above you, water casts
itself ecstatically and sings in tumbling
notes to land near your smitten gaze.

Of all you see and hope to pen, you are
the sight I came to see. The rest are gifts
of love to you from Me. And I am thrilled
when sunlight dances in your hair as pure
delight from you comes glancing back at me.

I love weddings. I think most of us do. They are the most joyful of gatherings. Hopes are high for the new couple. Smiles and laughter are plentiful. The bride and groom are looking their best…He, so handsome…She, so beautiful. Future dreams shine from their eyes. We celebrate their joy with feasting and dancing. The wine flows. Those of us long married are carried back to "our" time when love was shiny and new and so were our dreams. I am also carried forward in anticipation toward another celebration…the wedding day when Christ will consummate our betrothal to Himself. Our humble earthen forms will be raised up with Him in a beauty and Holiness that our weddings here below can only barely hint at. We wait for You to come for us, your beloved bride, riding on a white horse to take us home to be with You forever. I think something in every human heart longs for this marriage with our Creator. We may not even understand this longing but know that some sacred symbol is happening between a couple as they marry that calls this yearning forth in a place deeper within than we are aware of.

Hosea 2:19-20 And I will betroth you to me forever; I will betroth you to me in righteousness and in justice, in steadfast love, and in mercy. I will betroth you to me in faithfulness and you shall know the Lord.

Isaiah 62:3 For your Maker is your Husband, and the Holy One of Israel is your Redeemer; the God of the whole earth He is called.

We Will

I search for one magnificent word,
a shiny sentence, if either could define,
this "Something" our souls
come dressed for and ready to witness.
It glistens, intricate like light
on silver web patterns, spun lovely and strong.
We come and lean in, poised on tiptoes
to peek through a Holy window.

Ragnar…Lydia…clothed in ceremony,
you share a glowing glimpse
of your sweet secret. Honored, we dignify
(mostly) ours and your delirious gladness
with songs, strings, speech and
ribboned offerings. Elated, we
feast and affirm your poised potential…
Strength and beauty dance, uniquely entwined.

September 17, 2011

I first heard the Old Testament account of the fates of these two sisters, Rachel and Leah, in the romantic years of my youth. Both sisters were married to the same husband, Jacob. However, Rachel was the chosen, loved one. Jacob worked for her father seven years to earn the privilege of her hand in marriage. At the end of that long wait, on his wedding night, the two sister's father tricked Jacob and sent Leah into the dark of the marriage night tent instead of Rachel. When morning came and he saw Leah, of course he was disappointed. Leah had no say in the matter. Unfortunately, she fell in love with Jacob too. So after another seven years of work to earn his choice (all the while married to the hopeful Leah), Rachel finally became Jacob's. Hard place for Leah to be. I always felt compassion for her plight. To be honest, I felt deeply sorry for her. This poem was birthed out of compassion as I tried to imagine (happily for her) the surprise she experienced when she crossed over into eternity and discovered God's deep, choosing love for her. I am so grateful He considers each of us so equally and passionately loved that He, too, labors for our hand. We only have to take hold of His outstretched offer.

No Rachels or Leahs

In spring I dreamed
                    between dances.
Barefoot and carefree,
                    soft curls bounced
and feet flew
                    toward a different fate
than I thought I knew
                    would take me.
Into whose white tent
                    would I be welcomed?
Whose bright eyes
                    would I delight?
From whose warm arms
                    would blossom my womanhood?

Summer came
                    and no soul held
my pondered hopes
                    but placed a cup
of bitter brew
                    in disappointed hands.
Twice betrayed
                    this bartered bride
was heavy baggage
                    in hands whose
dreams were elsewhere
                    whose arms were dutiful.
I searched for brightness
                    inside his eyes

but found only splintered reflections
                    of dreams scattered
behind that dull gaze.

Oh, I was gallantly poised
                    I gave him sons!
and for awhile in autumn
                    hope was a warm enough cloak
til truth swept in
                    and stole those threads
and left stooped shoulders
                    to shiver in winter's cold.

So, yes…I was unusually surprised
                    when this used up earthly
form dropped and I
                    stepped into drenching
light and walked toward
                    His waiting embrace.
My dreams were whole
                    in those deep eyes
and His delight
                    both held and chose.
Still I cherish
                    His choosing love.
No Rachels or Leahs with Him.
                    We each are His first love.

Lovesong

I cannot write this love song to You.
I do not know the language of angels.
I am limited to syllables. Human
toned utterings that do not have
the breadth nor depth to capture
a response to Your revealed Essence…
To Your touch upon my life.

Someday I will shout it, sing it,
fling it across the endless skies and
mountains of Your country.
It will be my home too.
For now, I must seek to say it
with my eyes, my hands, my mouth.
I must dance it with flesh feet…
waiting for final release.

Wedding Day

Behind this film of silk, I wait.
My eyes are bright and ready, like deep pools,
to catch His image when He comes at dawn or dusk.
I shyly tuck a loose strand of hair and smile.
Soon He will lift my veil and all will clearly see.

My gown is smooth and cool. Hand sewn
with threads of sacrifice by One who suffered
with every stitch executed to tailor this satin to my
being with folks and folds of soft flowing white…
strong and shimmering…bride of a King.

Isaiah 61:10 I delight greatly in the Lord; my soul rejoices
greatly in my God. For He has clothed me with garments
of salvation and arrayed me in a robe of (His) righteous-
ness as a bridegroom adorns his head like a priest, and as
a bride adorns herself with her jewels.

Revelation 19:6 Then I heard what sounded like a great
multitude, like the roar of rushing waters and like loud
peals of thunder, shouting: "Hallelujah! For our Lord God
Almighty reigns. Let us rejoice and be glad and give Him
glory! For the wedding of the Lamb has come, and His
bride has made her-self ready. Fine linen, bright and clean,
was given her to wear."

Praise be to Him.

I am thankful for a lifetime of inspirational input from fellow pilgrims who have (and are still) leaving a legacy of crafted words for we who are wired to receive this way. My list includes many many songwriter's (including my husband, Mark)as well as writers of prose and poetry. I am deeply grateful to them each who have brought deep insights into my sphere and influenced my life for the better. Mark, you have listened over and over to the same poems as I attempted to wade my way through each evolvement… you so often intuitively knew when words or lines did not feel right or were unclear and together we found a better "ring". I also must include the influence of a college English teacher who has long since passed on. William Shaw's baby was poetry and and his winter poetry workshops helped me begin to gather my scattered words from journals and napkins and odd scraps of paper into sorts of forms that could be read and at least somewhat understood by others. Thank you Mr. Shaw. Thank you cousin Ann for the many years of sharing dreams and insights. You are a deep well whose bottom cannot be found. Thank you my friend Jan for listening to my scratchings and for giving honest input and encouragement…and sometimes spirited debate. Thank you Sharon Mavis for hosting those writer workshops and for the help they were to many of us. Thank you cousin Kathy for lending me your expert advise as a life time English teacher who is used to critiquing and offering help to others . You helped me as we tossed ideas for change back and forth yet you have allowed me to be who I am in my writing attempts…a novice who loves to express the inexpressible in words as best as I can. I am grateful to my family…both blood and otherwise . We are all , in our imperfect but grateful ways, heading "further up and further in" together. I appreciate that we do not journey alone. Most of all, I am grateful to God who constantly speaks and longs for our responses.

Annette Andersen
PO Box 4214
Traverse City, MI 49685

*A*nnette lives in her house full of books (not a few being poetry) in Traverse City Michigan. Her husband, Mark, and their two felines, Charlie and Luke, also fit in with her around the shelves and piles. She loves movement in nature; Waterfalls, rolling waves, wind in poplars, pines, and birch trees. And she has loved the rhythm and flow of words since a very young age. She writes most when she finds herself at a loss for the words she wants to speak … so she writes often. It is her hope that you who also pick up poetry books and give them a chance, might in turn be inspired by her efforts to "express the inexpressible" like she has been inspired all her life through the gifting of others who have friended the pen. And for all your days and nights may you also "lean in" close enough to hear Him speak uniquely to you.

CPSIA information can be obtained
at www.ICGtesting.com
Printed in the USA
JSHW011022241219
3175JS00003B/8